If you and your family are going through financial and economic difficulties, this is in no way an accident or something that should be solely weighted on your shoulders alone. Your demise is a part of a systematic attack from powerful entities designed to break your will and make you subservient to the needs of a select few. This book will attempt to unlock some of the mysteries behind who these individuals are and what there main goal is.

Eric Jason Lattier

The Mabus Puppet Masters
The Concepts of World Jewish Domination

Eric Jason Lattier

This Book Will Change Your Life !

authorHOUSE®

AuthorHouse™
1663 Liberty Drive
Bloomington, IN 47403
www.authorhouse.com
Phone: 1-800-839-8640

First published by AuthorHouse 6/30/2011

ISBN: 978-1-4634-0490-1 (e)
ISBN: 978-1-4634-0489-5 (dj)
ISBN: 978-1-4634-0488-8 (sc)

Library of Congress Control Number: 2011909143

Printed in the United States of America

The Singular can beat the Plural when righteousness is on their side.

Eric Jason Lattier

To secure ourselves against defeat lies in our own hands, but the opportunity of defeating the enemy is provided by the enemy himself.

Sun Tzu

Only under extreme pressure can Diamonds be created, and you my friends are Diamonds.

Eric Jason Lattier

Dedication

I would like to dedicate this book to my Jewish friends, government officials, and especially my lawyer buddies that spoke with me and contributed to the writing of this book. Without you I would not have had the knowledge or the inspiration.

Table of Contents

Preface

I would like to start this book by stating that I am not a writer, scholar, or an intellectual. I am a Christian and a regular American citizen born and raised in the southern states. I have traveled most of my country and the world. I have met many people and been in situations, especially in Israel, Jordan, Syria, Egypt, and Lebanon that have brought me to the conclusions in this book. As someone who has worked in Iraq, Kuwait, and Afghanistan, I believe my opinion of events pertaining to Israel and the other nations in the Middle East are to be heard. Due to privacy concerns, some of my sources for this book cannot be revealed. The opinions in this book are mine alone and I do not represent the objectives of any other person or organization. All similarities to any other literature otherwise are accidental. This is an opinion based book.

Introduction *To the "Three percenters"*

This book is about how approximately 3% of the United States population has taken over, controlling the U.S. and the world at large.

What is Zionism?

Zionism is a movement on all fronts with an objective to put all Jews in positions of financial, military, and political power in an attempt to control a common Jewish world agenda. The bases of operation for Zionists are the United States of America and the State of Israel, but they are in every country and their power is felt globally to all.

Mabus

"Mabus" is described by the famed seer and alchemist Nostradamus as being the "Collective Antichrist" and the last and final one of them to attempt to initiate a new world order setting off a terrible sequence of events. The first two Antichrist being individuals, Napoleon Bonaparte and Adolf Hitler, the third is spoken of having come from the second and is represented as a group of people instead of one person. In Nostradamus' book "The Century" number 2, Quatrain 62, he has thought to mention the death of the head of the Collective Antichrist. He speaks of it only having the name of Mabus.

The Century II, Quatrain 62

Mabus will soon die, then will come,

A horrible undoing of people and animals,

At once one will see vengeance,

One hundred hands (maybe powers), thirst,

famine, when the comet will pass

Chapter I

Backdrop of The Three Percenters

Throughout history we have been taught in our public schools and churches that Jews have been unjustly treated and attacked by other cultures. But scientific history tells us a different story.

While I was visiting Egypt, I took a tour that included most of the major archeological sites in the country. As I went from town to town I was always accompanied by a tour guide and sometimes even multiple guides. Their job was always the same. Once I traveled into a town there was to be someone waiting for me at a train station, at the dock of a boat, or at an airport. They would then take me to where ever I needed to go, eat, or sleep. And every morning I would be taken to a new destination. First it was the Pyramids of Giza. Then to the National Museum in Cairo, The Valley of the Kings, Aswan (which I thoroughly enjoyed), and so on and so on. I won't go into much detail of everywhere I went in Egypt because that would take us way too far off track and I could write a whole other book on the subject. But I will say this, I went to many areas to see the tombs of ancient Kings and dead Pharaohs, Hieroglyphics of Alexander the Great and many others.

The ancient Egyptians saved and recorded everything and one point was brought to my attention by my tour guide. He said Eric, out of all the tombs and mummies of Kings, pets, and farm animals(yes they mummified cats, alligators, monkeys, cattle and everything else you can imagine), how many remains of slaves did you discover? I said what? He said you saw the tomb of Ramses the II, you saw the burial grounds around the great Pyramids and everywhere else that is of historical significance. You even saw pictures of foreign conquers like Alexander the Great and the tomb of a Knights Templar. But did you see one Jew? I said no. He said one Hebrew then? I said I'm not sure if we did see one or not because I wouldn't know what to look for(after while all those mummies start to look alike). He said, well I can tell you there has not been any DNA evidence found to connect the Jews in Israel with any bodies uncovered in Egypt. I said are you implying that the Bible is lying when it speaks about Moses and the Hebrew/Israelite slaves in the book of Exodus? He told me no I am not saying the Bible is lying, but what I am saying is that Moses and the Hebrews/Israelites are not related to the Jews that are in Israel today. He went on to explain to me that there should at least be a few artifacts and buried bodies around the Pyramids from the workers there that were of the dissent of those in Israel. But a last, nothing. After the tour guide and I parted ways I did think about our conversation and found it to be strange there was no evidence of the descendents of those that call themselves Jews in Egypt, but I decided to shrug off the discussion and research it later.

Chapter II

The Great
Deceivers

I 'd like to state that I am not Anti - Semitic nor am I a Zionist. I am a Christian and I approached the research for the writing of this book with an open mind. I was raised in a family that was pro- Israel. And because of our Christianity, like most in America, we always took the side of Israel over any of her enemies. My church taught me to tie the current state of the Jews with my Christianity. I was taught that the Jews were the chosen people of God and their success was directly linked to my salvation. I have since come to and awakening. I no longer believe that Israel should be given a blind pass to do whatever it pleases. For far too long we have turned a blind eye to an influx of possible crimes against humanity and economic fraud schemes. Now, I want to repeat I'm not a Muslim, or an Arab, but while in Israel have witnessed beatings by the Israeli police against Palestinians, though I personally didn't witness any violence against Jews by Palestinians in Jerusalem or Tel Aviv. An Australian friend of mine showed me photos of

Israeli soldiers walking on a catwalk and below them was a Palestinian food and craft market. The soldiers walked on what looked to be a metal grating on top of the market. In some places, in between grades there look to be a brown mush coming through. In a couple of places this brown mushy stuff looked to be in plies. Please forgive me and I don't want to gross you out but this story must be told. I was told by my friend and his girlfriend that the brown material that I was looking at was human feces. The couple had taken the photos and visited the West Bank a few days prior. They had flown into Israel with a group from their local church. My Australian buddy was documenting all that he saw in an effort to write a story for his church back home describing the trip. They told me that the smell of arrant feces was so pungent in some areas that you couldn't wipe it away. The couple stated that the Israeli soldiers routinely dumped their feces on the market below them. So that you, the reader, can have a firm understanding of what I saw on the photos I will tell you that in the market I saw quite a few people, and stands of cheese for sale, candy, and fruit. Now can you imagine trying to self food at your little stand while having Jewish feces thrown on you? The couple told me that if that sounds and looks rancid, that I could surely trust them in believing it truly was.

Another story that I heard while I was there was that the Israelis had bombed a town close to or inside the Gaza Strip. Inside the war heads of the missiles the Israelis loaded a chemical called White Phosphorus(you may look up the effects of this chemical if you are so pleased to do so). The Israelis put out reports that they had previously been shot at with hand-held rockets. But what was not being reported on and what made the Israeli missiles so unique is that when fired they would explode about 30 feet in the air and disperse the white phosphorus throughout the area. Once it comes into contact with humans from the air it leaves severe chemical burns to all exposed areas of the body. It can burn all the way to the bone if someone is exposed for an extended period of time. Although White phosphorus is not illegal to use by treaty for most countries, it is rarely ever used because it strikes indiscriminately hurting all in the area including women and children. The Israeli Navy also recently attacked and killed some aid-volunteers that were attempting to take food and supplies to the people of the Gaza Strip. Also, there have been numerous reports of questionable Mossad activities inside Israel and abroad.

The Mossad is the equivalent to the U.S. CIA except they are thought to be more violent and less scrupulous. Many have seen the reports on the internet of unsolved murders, assassinations, and suicides that people have linked back to the Israeli Mossad. When they are involved there is usually no physical proof of their involvement, but the coincidences and timing of their acts are usually too large to ignore. They are stories of Mossad agents in every country of the globe killing politicians, media writers, television personalities, financial institution executives, religious figures, military personnel, and just everyday middle-class people in an attempt to further the Jewish Zionist agenda around the world. And who can forget the latest story in the U.S. of an Israeli terrorists who was allegedly killing and stabbing regular everyday people in Michigan and Ohio. After committing his crimes, the Israeli terrorist was captured by police trying to catch a flight out of the United States back to Israel.

I personally have been spit upon while I was in the Jerusalem for <u>no apparent </u>reason when I was walking with a tour group. There was also a couple there who seemed to be following extremely close and constantly sneezing on me. When I would turn around to look at them they would back away for a time, but then a few moments would pass and they would be there again almost touching me and sometimes actually doing so. This encounter with the couple caused me to be physically ill for three days by the way. To this day I don't know why. Also, at that time, I was in the old city walking to the Jewish quarters and I was constantly being badgered for my money by vendors when I would walk past a shop. I even had one shop owner curse at me because I wouldn't buy anything.

Also, on my first trip to Israel in 1996, as I was at the airport getting ready to fly out of the country to return back to the United States, I was asked by military personnel why I had flown into Israel on a one-way ticket and was exiting on a one-way ticket a month later. I explained to them that I had set my travel plans that way because I wasn't sure how long I would stay in their country. If I liked it, I planned to stay longer, if not I would leave beforehand. I was attempting to prevent myself from paying for a return ticket and reserving it for a day that I didn't want to leave on, and subsequently having to pay a penalty if I decided to change it, that wouldn't have been cost-effective for me. I was told by the military police that was okay, but that I couldn't leave the country for another 24 hours without further explanation from them.

So while I was sitting down at the airport trying to figure out where I wanted to go for the next 24 hours and in what hotel I planned to stay in, a flight attendant approached me. The young lady set down beside me. After about five minutes of small talk and introductions, she asked me for my phone number and my address so she could keep in contact with me while I was home in the United States. I was immediately taken aback by her suddenness to ask for my personal information after such a short time of being acquainted. But being that I was single, she was an attractive woman, and she seemed to be flirting with me I accepted her offer. I explained to her that I didn't have an address to give to her at that moment because I had recently moved out of my home in Louisiana and had placed all of my belongings in storage. I gave her my pager number and told her she could page me anytime and I would call her back as soon as I could. She said okay and we both went our separate ways. Well, after I returned to the United States, I moved to a new city which was Dallas, Texas and got a new apartment. I had not heard from or spoken to that flight attendant since that first encounter and approximately one week had past. It was at that time that I received a letter from the flight attendant postmarked from Israel. I had not even given my parents or anyone for that matter my new address so I was again taken aback. The letter was polite and nice. It stated that she would like to visit me if she ever came to the U.S. and that she wanted me to write her at the return address if I ever planned on returning to Israel. She stated that she didn't want to talk on the phone but wanted us to write one another. I was so weirded out by her writing me to a new address that I had just moved to. I decided not to correspond back to her. I thought to myself, who was that really and why would they be interested in little old me? Then I began to wonder, if someone was watching me. I contacted a friend of mine who had recently taken a job at a government intelligence agency and he told me that this would be off the record, but that the Israeli government has many Jewish and non-Jewish agents spying in the U.S. and periodically monitoring specific targets here. I said targets? What does that mean? He told me that many in Israel view the U.S. as an extension of their own country and they just would like to know what their little sister was doing over here at all times. I asked him, why would they want to monitor their allies in the U.S. (remember this is in 1996, pre-9/11)? He gave me no answer.

Chapter III
Diabolical

As I mentioned before, the knife slashing killer from Detroit was one of the most notoriously vicious criminals in United States history. But he is just one of many, in a string of some of the worst morally deprived people that are of Jewish and/or Israeli descent that has spread financial havoc and criminal chaos throughout the country over its' existence. It has been argued that Jews have affected our economic system negatively more than any other group in the country. Now you might say that's impossible, we never hear about that on the news. Then I will ask you a question. If you were the CEO of a powerful new station, and your cousins ran the other news stations, would you report honestly about the crimes committed by your cousins on a daily basis? Maybe you would reported it truthfully, but that's because you are a morally good person. Most Jews don't. They control the talk shows and news airwaves. If they are not the hosts themselves, they are the producer's, editors, etc.... and I can assure you they don't like to report the constant crimes committed by other Jews. And don't even mention Hollywood films. Unless you're Jewish, or you go out of your way to cater to Jews, you're probably not going to work in Hollywood. A friend of mine who was a screenwriter told me that your script wouldn't even get read or seen by anyone unless it portrayed Jews in a positive manner. But maybe it is a coincidence that some of the most diabolical criminals to ever be in this country have been Jewish. And to refresh your memory here they are:

The Jewish Dictionary
The Contributions of "Gods Chosen People" to our Society

Bernard Madoff - He is an ex- chairman of the NASDAQ stock market. He has admitted to de- frauding and bilking human beings out of 18 billion dollars using a Ponzi scheme that he developed through his investment firm. Many Jews have been accused of usury throughout history but a Ponzi scheme is just a little different type of fraud, so just to refresh your mind, a Ponzi scheme is defined as scam that promises investors high rates of return with very little risk. It uses money taken from new investors to pay the old ones without ever taking in any real profits. The scam can continue for years as long as it is not found out that are no real profits being generated and you continue to bring in new investors. Bernard Madoff ran one of the biggest ones in U.S. history. He was sentenced to 150 years in prison.

Scott Rothstein - Another Ponzi scheme operator and Ex-CEO of a law firm. It is estimated that he stole billions from people.

Robert J. Stein Jr. - The U.S. military allowed him to be employed as a comptroller for the CPA - Coalition Provisional Authority in Iraq. He was supposed to be providing oversight on a multi- million dollar reconstruction project. American taxpayers help fund that Iraqi government group and Mr. Stein stole millions and reportedly had money smuggled back into the U.S.A. in suitcases.

Franklin Moses - Ex- Governor of South Carolina and securities and tax thief. He sold 6 million in fake state securities

Joel Steinberg - He systematically and sadistically beat his wife and murdered a child that he illegally adopted. The details of the crime are to evil from me to put into print.

David Berkowitz - A.K.A. The Son of Sam. A deranged serial killer the terrorized New Yorkers. His method of operation was killing someone and then sending odd letters to the police. He was sentenced to six life sentences. Although the Berkowitz story remains popular his crimes were not as many as our recent Israeli born knife killer from Michigan, the total of his victims almost numbered to 20. Berkowitz' number of victims only numbered to13.

Joseph Seligman - He started his own bank called J.&W. Seligman& Co. It has been written about that he and a man named Jay Gould should be credited with creating the " Black Friday" stock market crash which lead to the Great Depression. He is also credited by some with causing the first Panama Canal Project in the 1800's to fail.

Leopold and Loeb - They were two teen age boys that killed another boy solely because they felt they were superior to him. They were privileged and brought up wealthy. They committed the murder and saw it only as a game to be played between themselves.

Samuel Byck - He attempted to Hijack an airliner and tried to have it flown into the White House to kill President Nixon in 1974.

Meyer Lansky - One of the biggest gangsters if not the

biggest in U.S. history. He controlled an illegal gambling empire that spread across the entire country. He was an associate of Charles Luciano and Bugsy Siegel. Lansky is rumored to having been involved in the murder of Siegel after he was unable to pay off a debts stemming from the construction of his Las Vegas hotel " The Flamingo". The Flamingo was the first Casino in Las Vegas. Lansky had strong ties to the Italian Mafia and is even rumored to have been the head of a mafia crime syndicate for a time.

Mickey Cohen - An associate of Meyer Lansky sent to Las Vegas to watch Siegel. He was instrumental in developing illegal sports gambling.

Abe Reles - A killer and Co- founder of an organization called Murder Inc. Murder Inc., was a group that specialized in murder for hire. Reles was one the groups biggest hit men.

Martin Goldstein - murderer and partner with Abe Reles.

Dutch Schultz - A notorious gang member and bootlegger in the New York City area.

Jim Levy - A cowboy, thief, and a murderer during the days

of the old west. He is rumored to have been in the famous town of Tombstone for a while.

Harry Strauss - A foot soldier and one of the biggest murderers involved in the group Murder Inc.

The Sugar House Gang - Also known as the " The Purple Gang", was a gang of Jewish thieves that specialized in armed robbery. They were rumored to have been involved in the famous St. Valentines Day Massacre and were suspects in the disappearance of the Lindbergh baby.

Jack Zelig - Gang member, murderer, and crook. He became the leader of the infamous Monk Eastman Gang. The gang specialized in prostitution and illegal gambling.

Max Zwerbach - Gang member and friend of Jack Zelig. He became the leader of the Monk Eastman Gang and also went by the name of "Kid Twist".

Vera Figner - She was an agitator, she is famous for participating in the planning of the assassination attempt on the Russian Tsar Alexander II.

Fanya Kaplan - She was also known as an agitator in Russia and she attempted to assassinate Vladimir Lenin.

Although she shot Lenin, he would recover and live on for years, but the damage left from the shooting is thought to be responsible for the multiple strokes suffered by Lenin, eventually causing his death a few years later.

Chapter IV

The Tyranny of the 3% that led to The Question

The Jewish people have been attempting to integrate into countries, cultures, cities, and towns around the world. But Jews have been at odds with the majority of the citizens in the world since the beginning of time, or at least since biblical times. Most Jews seem to object to forming coalitions with other groups of people around the world, even though they like to live amongst them in their countries to make money, they seem to be in constant conflict with whomever they come in contact with. Whether this is done on purpose or is accidental, it seems that most Jews are content to continue down the same road without reason, reflection, or regard for anyone other than themselves and there own financial well being. What I will try to do in this chapter is show you how the Jewish influence has affected the world as a whole.

After World War II the Allies implemented a plan to institute the state of Israel. So, in 1948 the Allied forces allowed the Jews to have their own state. At that time, the Europeans that call themselves Jews told Europe and everyone around the world that they were the descendents of the biblical Hebrews. The Jews also told us, because they are the chosen people, the land given to them should be in the exact location noted for the country of Israel in the Bible. And so it seems the process began to consolidate land for the Jews. Or did it begin at that time? Did the state of Israel began it's existence only after World War II? Were these people truly the descendents of Hebrews? Why had they been persecuted and told to get out of every country in Europe?

In 1933 Germany was in an economic crisis similar to the financial epidemic in the U.S. today. Banks were failing, manufacturing was stagnant, food was scarce, and soup kitchens started popping up all around the country. Unemployment was over 10%. Corruption in the upper levels of government and corporations ran rampant because of Jewish control. There was no such thing as fair commerce in Germany. The Weimar Republic was in full effect. Also, crime was at its highest levels. There were deaths, murders, and confidence schemes. It had been said that it was noticed the majority of crimes were being committed by Jews. The Jews had also been accused of committing a series of rapes of German women around the country. Inflation was at the highest points it had ever been. The German monetary note wasn't worth the paper was printed on. As the world looked on, Germany's problems were blamed on the reparations that had to be paid back to the international community(specifically France, Russia, The United States and the rest of the Allied forces). The reparations were enacted as a punishment to the Germans for infrastructural damage done during World War I and they were blamed for the entire war as a whole. The name of the document that enforced the reparations was called the Treaty of Versailles. Another damaging aspect of the Treaty to the German economy was that the majority of German exports would be stopped. Germany seemed not to be able to pay back the debt. In Germany there was mass political unrest. Jews were being charged with sedition and usury because of their actions during World War I. During the major political election between the Communist Party of Germany and the National Socialist Party of Germany(The Nazis), the Communist party lost to the National Socialists. Even though there were no major ideological differences between the two parties, Adolf Hitler and the rest of the Nazis on the right, said that the Bolshevik Russian Jews were the cause of Germany's loss during WWI. And next, the Nazis took control mainly because there were charges from them that Jewish and Russian spies controlled the German Communist Party. There was widespread disrespect felt by the German people from Jewish French soldiers that came in to the country to pick up the reparations checks. There have been reports that the Jewish French soldiers would make the German people on the street kiss their boots and even the ground in an attempt to purposely embarrass them. The treaty had also outlawed the rights of Germany to have a military and bear arms, so they were defenseless to protect themselves against any aggression from the soldiers. Most history books neglect to give you the reader any factual reasons for the Jewish-German conflict during World War II. You are always told that the war against the Jews was irrational and no further explanation was necessary other than that the Nazis and all of the German people at large were crazy. That's not true. The biggest complaint in Germany and all over Europe was that the Jews were taking advantage of them by the means of Usury. The Jews were notorious for lending money to non-Jews at extremely high interest rates that were most of the time illegal. This practice was echoed all over Europe at that time to be despicable and almost exclusively perpetrated by Jews . These events are rarely mentioned when the historical account of this time period is given. But I can assure you, inside Germany at that time there was a different story going on.

Most Germans noticed that all of the bank frauds, confidence schemes, and government looting were being committed and supported by one group of people - the Jews. And the Jews, as they call themselves seemed to be the problem and this issue had spread throughout the neighboring countries as well. It was also noticed that a high percentage of rapes in specific areas of the country were being committed by Hasidic Jews. Germany was divided, at odds with themselves. As I've stated, at that time most of the country was controlled by Jews. Most of the banks were owned by Jews. Also a new technology, picture movies and the theaters that showed them, were also all owned by Jews. Most grocery stores and factories were also Jewish owned. So as the country suffered and its people with it, most noticed that the only people still prospering were the Jews. How could this be? Why weren't they effected as well? And one night in January, there had been a report of the rape and murder of 12 German women at the hands of a group Jews in a parlor/ bath house.

Some German leaders were quoted as saying, "The people of Germany were helpless in the face of Jewish tyranny". Also, there had been rumors of Jews attempting to set up a sort of apartheid system in Germany. It would exist by Jews controlling the German population by the means of production and all economic points in between. It was at this time that Germany declared war with the Jews inside Germany and worldwide. The rest of the story is as they say, history.

Chapter V

The Flower Wars The Israeli Effect on the United States Military and Foreign Policy

Over the last 70 years Israel has done a terrific job of blending there foreign policy interests with those of the United States. Their plans have worked so well, that today, Israeli interests are American foreign policy and the United States military, when you get right down to it, are fighting the wars for Israel. As I've stated before, it has become inappropriate to speak evil of Israeli influence in America. Israeli lobbyist have made their agenda Americas agenda. Many countries have their people come into the U.S. to try to influence Americans to help them in some capacity. Americans understand that, and don't naturally see that as an issue. The only exception to that rule is Israel. Because of laws instituted with the help of Israeli lobbyists, all of their government agents don't register as foreign agents when they arrive in the U.S. and influence U.S. policy secretively. So there are many people in the U.S. that work secretively like spies throughout the country. You talk to them every day thinking they are fellow citizens of your country, but they are not. It has been reported that the different Congressional Israeli lobbying groups in Washington DC are the strongest in the country. Let's show how they have affected the world.

Jews in the U.S. and in the state of Israel have affected every war since World War II. Because the Germans, Poles, French, and most other European countries wanted them out of their nations we joined the war to help the Jews. Most people only know about the Germans wanting Jews out of their country, but the same was true in almost every European country. All of these countries were having economic problems caused by Jewish immorality and unscrupulous business practices. That's how all of the Jews ended up in the work camps. All nations pitched in to help to send them there. Think about it, there weren't enough German troops to take millions of Jews to work camps and fight the war abroad at the same time. No one wanted Jews in their country throughout Europe at that time.

The Korean and Vietnamese wars were actually started because of some of the same issues. We have been told that these wars were started to stop Russia and the spread of Communism. Not necessarily true. Think about it, how many Russians died in Vietnam and Korea? None to the best of my knowledge, one person on vacation maybe at the wrong time. Neither of these wars were about Russia or Communism as much as they were about Russians and other Communist countries not wanting to do business with the Jews because of the fear of being cheated and used. Israeli and American Jewish lobbying groups then began a war campaign to instill a Jewish style form of capitalism in the countries so they could do business there using the American military and lives as pawns for their dirty game. Because of the Jews, Russia and the U.S. ceased to be allies and the "Cold War" began. Israel was also the cause of the Cuban missile crisis. Yes, the missiles in Cuba pointed at the U.S. were Russian, but what has just been revealed by Cuban intelligence records is that the missiles were originally bought by the Israelis from Russia. They were illegally armed with nuclear material, and then sold to Jewish Cuban officials in the Castro government in an attempt to start a war between the U.S. and Russia. The war would then remove the U.S. and Russia as superpowers and bring Israel closer to a Zionist world order and Jewish global dominance.

The first Gulf war in Iraq - some of the same. At the time, Kuwait had a secret agreement with Israel for oil at rock-bottom cost in exchange for Israeli military weapons. It was during that time that Iraq invaded Kuwait in an effort to corner the oil market and break up the oil deal with the Israelis. Then Israel ordered President Bush(number 41) to attack Iraq and restore Kuwait as to not disrupt their financial energy interests.In 2003, there was a second Gulf War with Iraq. Israeli Mossad agents provided American intelligence agencies with information about Iraq possessing Weapons of Mass Destruction(WMD's) . Israel and their oil lobbyists told President Bush(number 43) to attack Iraq again and sale the war as a necessary tool to promote U.S. national interests against WMDs. No WMDs were ever found inside Iraq. It has been rumored that Israel planned to plant WMDs inside Iraq but never found an opportunity to do so because there were too many international inspectors around the country that were in the way.

The war with Afghanistan was an extremely necessary one. Osama bin Laden and his organization Al Qaeda orchestrated the attacks on the World Trade Center and killed thousands of Americans. The Taliban, the ruling government in Afghanistan at the time, refused to turn over and tell the exact whereabouts of bin Laden so the war was imminent. But what most don't know are the real reasons bin Laden and Al Qaeda started a war with the U.S. Americans were told that it was because Al Qaeda hates our freedom. Then it was Muslims hate our freedom. Then Islam hates our freedom. That's just not true. Being someone who has traveled to many Muslim nations and spent a lot of time with Arabs, I can tell you that they love American television shows, sports, and music. And when you ask them what country they would like to live in other than their own, most if not everyone's first choice is the United States of America. The real reason that Osama bin Laden, Al Qaeda, the Taliban, Iran, Syria, Lebanon, Egypt, and most other Muslim nations gives when asked why they dislike the U.S. is because of our blind, unequal, financial, and military support of Israel against the Palestinians. And that's just a fact my friends whether it is a popular one are not. Israel's newest war that it wants American troops to fight and die for is against Iran. Iran is close to finishing a nuclear weapon and is afraid that Israel will attack them. Israel is attempting to get the U.S. to attack Iran even though the Iranians are not a direct threat to the U.S. Israel would rather the U.S. fight the war against Iran instead of them doing it so that there would be no Israeli military personnel lost. The President of Iran has stated that "Israel is a threat to the world" and that he would "like to wipe Israel from the face of the map." He also has stated that "the only way to defeat Israel is for all the Arab countries to work together on this problem and to bomb the state from within and without." These are the wishes of Iran.

Chapter VI

The Syrian, Iranian, and Venezuelan Connection

Iranian Nuclear Technology, Border Security, and Illegal Immigration - These issues have dominated the headlines in the last few days, but there's one story that combines these issues into one possible story on which most in the media have not reported .

While the debate over illegal immigration and border security continues in our country, most in the media and the majority of Americans are focusing on the 14th amendment and what to do with the "illegal's" that are already in within the United States. We all could possibly be missing an impending threat due to our current foreign policy in relation to the country's of Venezuela and Iran and the lax security on our southern border.

In Iran, Russia is in the process of fueling Iran's nuclear reactor as we speak. This act has left the United States and Israel on edge due to the nature of the relationship between the countries at this current time. At present, the United States does not have an active diplomatic role in any peace talks between Iran and Israel. Tensions between the two countries have steadily risen within the last two years. During the last Bush administration and the current Obama administration, U.S.- Iranian relations have been virtually nonexistent due to a lack of willingness to interact with Iran and its present leader President Mahmoud Ahmadinejad from the U.S. State Department. This rift, has lead Ahmadinejad to accuse the U.S. of playing favorites between themselves and the Israelis which has only added fuel to an already tense relationship. The U.S. has demanded that Iran tone down its' rhetoric against Israel before any talks can take place. Israel is reportedly considering an air strike against Iran s' nuclear facility in Bushehr, a town about 700 miles south of Tehran.

In Venezuela, in the latest episode in a comedy of errors between two countries, President Hugo Chavez has accused the U.S. of backing rebels inside Venezuela and Columbia against his government in an attempt to over throw him and install a new regime. The U.S. has repeated denied any role in a scheme against Venezuela and has refused any one-on-one talks with the President after it levied accusations of possible human rights violations against his government.

From Caracas, Venezuela, Hugo Chavez has initiated

an agreement with the countries of Iran and Syria that will benefit all three countries militarily and economically, but how their new found friendship will affect the United States and its relationship with these three countries has yet to be determined.

In 2007, the first of many flights originating in Tehran, with a brief stop in Damascus, Syria, before continuing onto Caracas took place to form a new economic and military pact. Under the terms of the agreement between the countries, in a nutshell, Venezuela and Syria agree to support each other with advanced missile technology, Iran and Venezuela agreed to assist Syria in upgrading its oil refining capabilities, and both Syria and Iran agree to purchase gasoline from Venezuela. But what really makes the U.S. and Israel uneasy is that Venezuela has reportedly agreed to allow the exploration and exportation of Uranium to Iran from the deposits of its country.

Under the current agreement Iran has with Russia and the International Atomic Energy Agency (IAEA), Iran can only use its nuclear energy from the Bushehr plant for domestic electricity. If fully operational, the plant could support the energy needs of the majority of the country. Iran is obligated to give all used reactor fuel from the Bushehr plant to the Russians as so to extinguish the possibility of nuclear proliferation. Used reactor fuel can be used to produce Plutonium which could then be used to complete an atomic weapon. The fear is, using its alliance with Venezuela, Iran could circumvent IAEA inspections and its' "no proliferation" deal with Russia. Iran could purchase, produce, and enrich Uranium without the knowledge of the IAEA and could potentially begin to weaponize nuclear material. Uranium, has to be more than 90% enriched to be at weapon grade level to produce a nuclear warhead. The current fuel provided by Russia is at 3.5% which is way below the weapon grade level needed. However, Uranium supplied from Venezuela to Iran could be much more difficult to track and test for the IAEA and the international community.

Also, one of the main concerns from U.S. intelligence agencies is that they are having a hard time finding out who's coming in and out of Venezuela on these flights from Tehran. These flights land at a military base in Venezuela. No one is allowed to book seats on these flights. The flights always show no availability and there is no flight manifest to show the names of the persons that are flying in and out of Venezuela.

Eric Jason Lattier

As the perception from most Arab nations that the United States continues to support Israel's foreign policy unevenly in the Middle East when it concerns Palestinians, Israel's perceived enemies and other nations continue to pull away from the U.S. Mideast policy. This perception of the U.S. in the region, could make radicals from the Middle East, attempt to board one of the flights into Venezuela from Tehran and make their way from South America into Mexico and across the border into the U.S. - to possibly conduct terrorist activities.

Chapter VII

Power by Persuasion and Infiltration

Almost working like a government law enforcement agency, Jews have infiltrated many political, civil rights, and labor organizations. Although a lot of the groups they target are mainstream political parties, some are fringe groups. While the purpose of the Zionists in American political parties is to influence and push forward a pro-Jewish and Israeli agenda, their purpose in civil rights and fringe groups is to control, marginalize, and suppress.

Within Black civil rights organizations, Jews have always sought control. By supporting and planting individuals in positions of leadership, Zionists have been successful in structuring Black policy and controlled the economy of historically Black neighborhoods and institutions. The African-American community has always been a staple part of the Jewish American financial scheme. Throughout the 1900s and into the 2000s Jews have owned the majority of businesses that cater to the needs of African Americans. Whether it is the corner grocery, the neighborhood bank, or the latest rows of ghetto project apartments and homes, Jews have always owned them. Laundromats, medical clinics, and restaurants also are majority owned by Jews. Especially in the 1900s, Jews quickly learned that blacks were treated as second-class citizens and Jews began to exploit that to their advantage. Throughout most of the century, Blacks were in a struggle for civil rights receiving little or no support from other ethnic groups and minorities, Blacks had only themselves to stick to and were at an educational and financial disadvantage to others. Jews figured out a way to keep White Americans as their friends by using Christianity and the Old Testament connections as leverage. With Blacks, they convinced them that they were the only friends they had and not to trust anyone else. Jews then convinced community leaders to allow them to exclusively build stores and projects, implementing a series of controls whereby the only way for upward mobility was through Jewish ties. Jews then paid and supported these hand picked Blacks for leadership positions to keep this process going.

Jews then turned their attention to the unions. This was a more powerful economic force that would eventually propel them to lobbying Congress and taking over the production of movies in Hollywood. Once Jews established themselves in positions of authority by only hiring their own, they controlled the agendas and took over. To this very day Jews dictate what actors get hired, what movies get financed, and which scripts get accepted in Hollywood.

In industry, they have taken over the leadership roles in auto and teachers unions. Most Americans blame them for the auto industries decline.

Chapter VIII
Monitoring

After WWII, Jews began to infiltrate many fringe organizations like the Nazi Party U.S.A., Communist Party U.S.A., and many churches in the United States. The purpose was to monitor activities and create dissension. They work almost like a spy agency, changing their names so they won't sound Jewish and marrying Caucasians so they would have the appearance of being white. By doing this they have become masters of disguise.

Also, some reports have stated on the internet that some Jewish rights groups have influenced companies to purchase their software so that everyone's internet activities can be monitored and the information filtered to Israel for processing. Working like puppet masters over these groups and the general population as a whole, the Jews have become the most powerful secret society in the world.

Chapter IX

Banking

Most Americans, if not all are familiar with the world banking crisis. With the failing of a huge percentage of banks in the United States and around the world, people are wondering how all this happened. Well it started like this, the Zionists are reportedly on their last leg of preparations toward the formation of a new Jewish world order. They came up with a plan to destroy the world banking systems excluding Israels' in an attempt to drive the entire world to become dependent on Israeli owned banking, trading, mortgage, insurance, and lending institutions. How to go about doing this? Well, first they had to influence the United States government, and they had a friend in G.W. Bush. During his Presidency, G.W. Bush was ordered by Israeli and American Jews to deregulate the banking industry. The Jews' puppets in Washington on Capitol Hill were then told to force all banks in the U.S. to start doing more lending(the Jews thought that if you destroy the American banking system first, the rest of the world's banks would follow).

Then the Zionist ordered every bank under their control (which was the majority of them) to start giving out sub-prime B-paper loans. The loans would be structured so that they would almost be impossible to pay back with extremely high interest rates and have balloon payments at the end of most of the years. Does this almost sound like usury to you? The Jews convinced the world banks that even if people defaulted on their loans they would still get their money back. The banks were then supposed to foreclose on the property and resale it keeping the equity gained from the previous owner. And we all know what happened next. Foreclosed properties sat vacant for months, the job market declined, and the housing market bubble burst causing the biggest financial market bailout in U.S. history.

Chapter X
Religion
The Mabus Doctrine

In the Holy Bible the book of Revelation chapter 2, versus 8 and 9, they have been called "the synagogue of Satan".

> *To the angel of the church in Smyrna write:*
> *These are the words of him who is the First and*
> *the Last, who died and came to life again. I*
> *know your afflictions and your poverty--yet you*
> *are rich! I know the slander of those who say*
> *they are Jews and are not, but are a <u>synagogue</u>*
> *<u>of Satan</u>.*

God calls them people who say they are Jews who are really not. After World War II there was no way genetically to tell those that called themselves Jews from Europeans.

The "so called Jews" of that day said it was because the Jew had done so much race mixing with the Europeans that there was not a difference between them anymore. After World War II, Americans and the British just took their word for it that they were Jewish(there was no real way to tell at that time). Hitler and the Nazis said that these people that are calling themselves Jews now went by many different names in their country and they were in no way the descendents of the Hebrews from the Bible. He said that they were merely degenerate thieves feasting on work of others. The Bible also infers that these people speak that they are the "chosen ones" and are good, but in their actions they will be worse than everyone else. Jews today around the world per capita are the most criminal group of people on this planet. As previously stated most white collar crimes are committed by Jews. Where the person who robs the local gas station only affects the people in the store and in the immediate area -The Jew that uses his job to rob banks, corporations and governments, affects every person in the entire world and it sometimes takes decades to fix. Throughout the Bible, God chooses a group of brave people to stand up against these "false Jews" and remove them from these countries so there would be peace and harmony again.

Also in the Bible, they have been referred to as the antichrist and "the abomination that causes desolation." the Bible speaks of the false Jews in many books, chapters, and versus.

The book of Daniel, Chapter 9, verse 26 says:

After the 62 'sevens,' the Anointed One will be cut off and will have nothing. The people of the ruler who will come will destroy the city and the sanctuary. The end will come like a flood: War will continue until the end, and desolations have been decreed. He will confirm a covenant with many for one 'seven.' In the middle of the 'seven' he will put an end to sacrifice and offering. And on a wing of the Temple he will set up an <u>abomination</u> <u>that</u> <u>causes</u> <u>desolation</u>, until the end that is decreed is poured out on him.

Also…

The book of Daniel, Chapter 11, verse 31 says:

His armed forces will rise up to desecrate the temple fortress and will abolish the daily sacrifice. Then they will set up the <u>abomination</u> <u>that</u> <u>causes</u> <u>desolation</u>. With flattery he will corrupt those who have violated the covenant, but the people who know their God will firmly resist him.

Also…

The book of Daniel, Chapter 12, verse 10 says:

> *Many will be purified, made spotless and refined, but the wicked will continue to be wicked. None of the wicked will understand, but those who are wise will understand. From the time that daily sacrifice is abolished and the <u>abomination</u> <u>that</u> <u>causes</u> <u>desolation</u> is set up, there will be 1290 days. Blessed is the one who waits for and reaches the end of the 1335 days. As for you, go your way till the end. You will rest, and then at the end of the days you will rise to receive your allotted inheritance.*

All of these verses speak of things that began to happen at the same time. Most believe the abomination that causes desolation prophesized about in the Bible is the state of Israel and its leadership today. Since its beginning in 1948, the state of Israel has been the cause of or has caused almost every single conflict and war in the world as I have already stated. Whether it's because of the Palestinian-Jewish conflict directly or indirectly, or their economic destructive power that always originates in the state, Israel is always the center.

The so called Jews all decided to attach their existence to Christianity. They figured out if they used words that came from the Bible to describe themselves they would become to be protected by the United States and all Christendom for that matter. These are all lies propagated by the perpetrators themselves as predicted in the Bible. The fictitious home of the so called Jew will always be the abomination that causes desolation according to the Bible. As a Christian, my Lord and Savior Jesus Christ spoke of them as well. Before we go any further, let us remember that it was the Jews that crucified and murdered our Lord and Savior Jesus Christ. As a cruel joke, a crown of thorns was placed on his head with only the words nailed above his cross "Jesus of Nazareth, the King of the Jews". The Jews at the bottom of the cross looked on with glee and laughed until they could no more at the plight of our Lord and Savior.

In the book of Matthew, Chapter 24, verses 14 to 16, they are spoken of:

> *And this gospel of the kingdom will be preached in the whole world as a testimony to all nations, and then the end will come. So when you see*

> *standing in the holy place 'the <u>abomination</u> <u>that</u> <u>causes</u> <u>desolation</u>,' spoken of through the prophet Daniel-- let the reader understand-- then let those who are in Judea flee to the mountains.*

Also...

In the book of Mark, chapter 13, verses 13 to 14 and says:

> *All men will hate you because of me, but he who stands firm to the end will be saved. When you see 'the <u>abomination</u> <u>that</u> <u>causes</u> <u>desolation</u>' standing where it does not belong-- let the reader understand-- then let those who are in Judea flee to the mountains.*

All these verses speak of the current day and the state of Israel. These verses call the Jews the abomination that causes desolation. As previously discussed, because of these Jews, wars against many nations are going on and encouraged today. Christ says, when you see them there get ready, change is coming. You may have to flee and you may be persecuted because of them. May God give us the strength.

In the book of Revelation beginning with Chapter 13, verse 18 and continuing through to Chapter 14, verse 5 it says:

> *This calls for wisdom. If anyone has insight, let him calculate the number of the beast, for it is man's number. His number is 666.*
>
> *Then I looked, and there before me was the Lamb, standing on Mount Zion, and with him 144,000 who had his name and his father's name written on their foreheads. And I heard a sound from heaven like the roar of rushing waters and like a loud peal of thunder. The sound I heard was like that of harpist playing their harps. And they sang a new song before the throne and before the four living creatures and the elders. No one could learn the song except the 144,000 who had been redeemed from the earth. These are those who did not defile themselves with women, for they kept themselves pure. They follow the Lamb wherever he goes. They were purchased from among men and offered as*

firstfruits to God and the Lamb. No lie was found in the mouths; they are blameless.

Okay, let's start with the last one first. In chapter 14 the Bible speaks of 144,000 that are saved. The so-called Jews have told us this chapter refers to them and references chapter 7, verse 1, as proof of that. Chapter 7 speaks on the 144,000 sealed by God from the 12 tribes of Israel. But there is no DNA evidence connecting them to the Hebrew 12 tribes of Israel in the Bible. And if you were to ask most, if not all truthful Rabbis which tribe they are descendents of, they would tell you that they don't know. Also the Bible states there are only 144,000 saved and sealed from the 12 tribes of Israel. To put that into context, there are millions of people who claim to be Jews today, 144,000 would not be a lot of them.

Okay, let's go back to chapter 13 verse 18. The Bible states that a man with wisdom will know the beast by a number which is also man's number - 666.

In ancient cultures including that of the Egyptian and some European ones, there has been something called "Satan's Hexagon." You may have also known it by its other name "The Ginnzsberg Hexagon". The Ginnzsberg Hexagon is the beginning of, and is at the center of a symbol that most of you know by another name, hiding its true meaning and purpose. I will attempt to illustrate this symbol for you. Here comes wisdom.

They are calling it the Star of David today.

6 - (The Center) The Ginnzsberg Hexagon

6 - (The Triangles) The Satanic Trinity

6 - (The Points of the Star) They represent
the six most powerful Elders of Zion.

The Center of the Star of David is really the Ginnzsberg Hexagon. The first 6 represents the six sides of the Ginnzsberg Hexagon. These are the 6 powers given to the Jews by Satan himself. The exact powers given are called "The Diabolical Gifts from Ginnzsberg (Satan). They are:

One - The power of Usury,
Two - The power of Perfect Deception through lies,

Three - The power to Enslave,

Four - The power of Indirect Murder,

Five - The power over Money,

Six - The power to make War

The second 6 is represented by the six triangles on the corners of the Star. These are the six places that have been and will come under the power of the Beast at different times in world history.

One - All Roman Entities

Two - All Germanic and Russian Entities

Three - All British and French Entities

Four - All Ottoman(This includes

Arab and African) Entities

Five - All Spanish Entities

Six - All American(This includes

The United States) Entities

The Three sides of the Triangle are called the Satanic Trinity(Or Unholy Trinity) - The Beast, False Prophet, and Satan (All are found in the book of Revelation)

The third 6 is represented by the six points(or tips) of the Star. The six points represent the six most powerful Elders of the Zionist movement that exercise control over the world. To this day, many have speculated, but their names and positions have not been proven. Most humans are taught to stay on guard and be watchful.

You got it right. The quote 'Star of David' is the symbol for the Beast and it equals mans number of 666.

Chapter XI

Sacrificial Lambs Israel Attacks the USS Liberty

On June 8,1967, 34 American military personnel were murdered in a cruel act of war that still to this day is rarely talked about or written about. In June of 1967, Israeli government officials traveled to America to inform U.S. government officials of their plans to attack Egypt over disputed borders. The Israelis thanked the U.S. for providing them with military weapons and training over the years. They wanted to know if the U.S. would help them with one more thing. The Israelis wanted the U.S. to join them in the war against Egypt and assist, so they could attack two other neighboring countries - Syria and Lebanon.

The U.S. refused to help the Israelis in this matter. The Israelis then asked if the U.S. would help attack Egypt then. The United States government informed Israel that the U.S. could not be involved in any way with this war due to the fact that American involvement could spark World War III. The Israelis were dissatisfied and very unhappy with the American response. They left the country informing

Jews within the government to keep a watchful eye on the Americans.

On June 5, 1967, Israel attacked Egypt with the military might given to them. The Israelis were winning the war, but what they truly wanted was the total destruction of Cairo and the leveling of the entire country of Egypt. To do that the Israelis needed help. No country in Europe or the Americas was willing to assist them with this. It was at this time when the Pentagon ordered the USS Liberty, a naval surveillance ship, to go sit in international waters in between the coasts of Egypt and Israel. Their orders were to use the ship's radio surveillance technology to listen to radio transactions involving Israel and Egypt.

On the morning of June 8, sailors on the USS liberty noticed Israeli jets circling them. The Jews circled the ship for some time and after awhile reportedly left. The sailors reported that they were not alarmed by the Israeli jets being there because the Jews were the allies of the United States. That afternoon the first of many missiles hit the Liberty. The Israeli fighter planes had returned and were now bombarding the ship with a massive aerial strike. At one point according to American sailors, Napalm was dropped on the deck of the ship. Sailors reported noticing strange markings on the planes. Saying that the warplanes looked to have similar markings to an Egyptian fighter jet but that the insignias were in the wrong place. The sailors also noted the planes were shaped and sounded like Israeli jets. The USS Liberty never fired back on the Israeli fighters being that it was a defenseless surveillance ship.

The final weapon leaved against the ship was a torpedo dropped from the aerial assault. The torpedo struck the side of the ship. The USS liberty would have surely sunk had it not been for the resolve and bravery of the sailors aboard doing whatever they possibly could to save the vessel. Israeli jets disappeared. Once S.O.S. messages had been received, and the Pentagon told of the attacks, the reports were that the fighter jets were Egyptian. The Israelis had sent these false reports out to the U.S. government in an attempt to get them to enter the war and attack Egypt. Authorization was given at that time from the U.S. government for another U.S. naval warship in the area to hit Cairo, Egypt with a nuclear strike. Two American fighter jets took off armed with nuclear missiles headed for Cairo. The Jewish plan for the U.S. to attack Cairo almost worked until a distant faint message was sent to the Pentagon from the USS Liberty. It was reported that the jets that attacked, sounded and looked Israeli by shape, but had Egyptian markings. The Pentagon immediately commanded the two U.S. warplanes to abort their mission and return back. The planes had been minutes from Cairo. After the U.S. first contacted the Israeli government, the Israelis denied any knowledge or involvement in the incident. It was only after the U.S. told them that they were in the process of decoding intercepted radio commands ordering the attacks that were thought to have originated in Israel, that the Israelis finally admitted involvement. They stated that the attack on the Liberty had been a case of mistaken identity. They claimed they thought the ship was an Egyptian war vessel. The Israelis to this day have never issued a public apology to the United States. The American media for some reason has never done any major extensive reporting on the incident. 34 American military sailors died that day in the attack. May God bless and allow the victims of that vicious attack on the USS Liberty to rest in peace. May we not let their sacrifice be in vain and punish those responsible for their murder. To this day no Israeli military personnel have been charged or prosecuted.

Chapter XII

Liberating Seth
The Jews in
Europe Today

A good friend of mine from Austria told me a story once. He said a few years ago in a small town, of which he did not name, a group of Jews killed a small boy named Seth that was trying to walk home. The Jews had been out drinking spirits and gambling at a brothel house when they encountered the small boy as he was trying to get home. After running an errand to the local store in an attempt to get items for his father, the Jews accosted him. As for the details of the attack, I'm not strong enough to write about what was told to me. My friend told me that as word spread about the brutal attack, anger against the Jews kindled. Most felt that this was the last straw. There were a lot of financial and media scandals at that time, all perpetrated by Jews, but now they were committing random acts of violence against small children. Six of the Jewish perpetrators were captured by police finally, and on the way to the police station they were stopped by group of angry citizens from the community. The citizens took the Jews from police and doused them with some flammable liquid, setting them on fire in the street. The people refer to this event as "Liberating Seth." Some saw this as an act of bravery against evil.

My fear is that this type of thing could happen all over again in Europe, due to our latest financial crisis. Crimes against humanity are up in certain areas, reportedly perpetrated by Jews. In France, Germany, Austria, Italy, Greece, and Great Britain there've been mumblings that the bubble could burst and violence could break out in the streets against Jews. Let's all hope this doesn't happen and pray for peace. Regardless of what it has been rumored the Jews have done, we are all taught as Christians to turn the other cheek and let the legal system take control of the situation. To my knowledge these are not isolated incidents. Feelings of hostility are running rampant throughout Europe. And the current financial crisis and world instability are not helping things at all.

Chapter XIII

The Arabs and Zionism

As many Arab organizations are meeting periodically around the world, the same topic comes up every time. The Palestinian-Israeli situation and Jewish World Zionism. A friend of mine who is Arab once told me that most, if not all Arab countries live in fear of a military strike from the Israelis at all times. They live in fear of Zionism and the threat that someday their country maybe invaded to provide land for Israeli Jews. I will explain to you what I've explained to my Arab friends. It seems to me, the only way to stop the advancement of the Zionists and their building plans throughout the Middle East, is for Arab nations to put up a unified front. All the Arab states must make a military pact. This must be a defense pact and an nonaggression pact for all members. Differences must be set aside for the common goal and task at hand. Sunni and Shia together. Divided you will fall. Syria and Lebanon must join in with the Gulf states. They must combine their resources. Pakistan and Iran must be a part of the group to give it validity. Syria, Lebanon, Egypt, Jordan, Kuwait, Saudi Arabia, Oman, Yemen, Qatar, UAE, Iraq, Libya, and the rest of the African states, etc.... You get the drift. I also have asked them some questions that I still have not gotten the answer too. Or, I haven't received an answer that makes total sense and gives a final solution to these questions involving Jews. I've always wondered, even with the current Palestinian-Israeli conflict, why do so many Jews live in Egypt, Syria, and Jordan peacefully? There are over 30 synagogue's in Egypt alone, and there are never any conflicts that I have heard of.

Also, if the President of Iran, Mahmoud Ahmadinejad is the Jew hating racist the media tells us he is, why does he allow Jews to live in Iran freely without incident? There are over 25,000 Jews living in Iran to date. These are questions I hope to someday get answers too.

Chapter XIV

Conspiracy Theories that put Zionists behind the Assassinations of Kennedy and MLK

There are conspiracy theories floating around out there in cyberspace and other places that state the Jews were behind the assassination plots of John F. Kennedy and Martin Luther King Jr. I will start with the Kennedy story first, only because I got it from an ex-military intelligence officer while I was overseas and I guarantee you haven't heard this yet. I have read books and documents that state Mossad agents in the U.S. hired Lee Harvey Oswald to assassinate President Kennedy. Also, that Jack Ruby, a Jew born Jacob Rubenstein, was an undercover Israeli agent. Jack Ruby subsequently killed Lee Harvey Oswald in an attempt to hide the truth. Jack Ruby was a strong supporter of Israel some reports say, and would have done anything to protect it. Mr. Ruby according to some, was possibly poisoned by the Mossad after it was thought that he might start to write a book telling the truth from his jail cell. The motive behind the assassination of Kennedy was reportedly because of Kennedy's absolute assertion that

Israel must never become a nuclear state. And that after tense correspondence between him and Israeli officials he sent nuclear inspectors and military personnel to Israel to impede and stop any progress the Israelis had in building a facility. Reportedly, Kennedy didn't want them to have the weapon because he never trusted those people with such technology. In certain circles it is accepted as fact that soon after the murder of President Kennedy. Israel became a fully functioning nuclear power.

The Assassination of MLK

Okay, before write this I want you to know that most of you are going to find it shocking what I'm about to reveal. Are you ready? Well, here it is even if you are not.

In 1996, on my first trip to Israel I was staying at a place called, "The Travelers Hostel" on Ben-Yehuda Street in Tel Aviv, Israel. It was there that I met a man by the name of Manaham(the spelling has been changed). Manaham was a senior aged Jewish fellow with gray hair that worked as a schoolteacher in Tel Aviv. He taught English there and we had many interesting conversations including the history of Israel and other intellectual subjects. Being that I'm always on a quest for knowledge, I listened intensely to his stories about Israeli life. He took me around to historic landmarks and cities, like Jaffa.

One day he told me he wanted me to see the memorial that was set up at the site of the assassination of the Prime Minister Yitzhak Rabin. As we walked past the site, he told me that he used to be a military official and he assisted with the investigation of the killer of Rabin. At that point, I moved the conversation into other matters concerning the Mossad and Israeli intelligence. We went to a tavern and had a few drinks as he explained how Israel had secret agents all over the world. It was at this time when he told me that he would let me in on a secret that he knew about concerning a man from my country. He asked me if I knew who a man by the name of Martin Luther King Junior was? I told him, yes of course I did. He then began to tell me how he came across and read some old intelligence documents while he was in the service about a Negro civil rights leader by the name of Martin Luther King Jr. He stated specifically that Mossad agents in the U.S. had been ordered to kill M.L.K. I sat at the bar in shock and disbelief at what I had just heard. He said it was about a 15 page document that stated consent had been given to go ahead with the assassination, but it did not say who the consent came from. No motive was ever given, only that the Mossad was cleared to assist in this matter. He told me that this document was in a file with other sensitive paperwork, and that he was not officially cleared to look at these documents in the first place. So outside from telling a couple of people, he kept his mouth shut. James Earl Ray, the man convicted of killing M.L.K., always stated that he didn't act alone all the way up to his death, telling anyone who would listen. But again we come back to the motive for Jewish involvement. We can only speculate on the details until more information comes forward. One theory is that James Earl Ray was contracted out by the Mossad on orders from individuals in the U.S. government. M.L.K. had been under surveillance for sometime. The operation was known as Cointelpro. Some members of the U.S. government at that time wanted to derail the civil rights movement and could have asked the Mossad to assist in this matter. Another theory is that the Jews in the U.S. had M.L.K. killed in an attempt to stop the civil rights movement because it was hurting Jewish owned businesses in the Black community. The Blacks during that time lived in ghettos. Ghettos were cramp housing areas originally set up by the Nazis to keep all of the Jews in one area during WWII in Germany. The Jews after coming to The United States decided to use the idea on the Blacks. Suppressive laws, such as Jim Crow laws, meant that Blacks could only go into certain areas. Mostly keeping them in a position to shop and work in the ghettos set up by Jews, Blacks were under their control. In these ghettos, almost all of the grocery stores, cleaners, and clothing stores, etc… were owned by Jews. The suppression of rights for Black Americans made a lot of money for the Jewish community for many years. The money would then be used to educate Jewish children and help make Jewish politicians and businesses go national. The advancement of Blacks and the M.L.K. civil rights movement would allow the Negroes to leave and move out of the ghettos. That was something that cost Jews a lot of money. The idea was that if they killed M.L.K., then the civil rights movement would die and blacks would be forced to stay under the control of Jews.

Chapter XV

A Brief Synopsis on The Protocols Of The Learned Elders of Zion

The Protocols of the Learned Elders of Zion is a book that was written from the minutes of a secret Jewish organization that controls the economics and political structures of every country on the planet. To be fair and unbiased, I would like to state that most Jewish groups say that this book is full of anti-Semitic lies. The first copy of the minutes was reportedly somehow intercepted by Professor Segei Nilus and published not too long thereafter. I will attempt to summarize and identify the key points and topics of the book.

To read a complete copy of the Protocols you can easily find it free online at many different websites. All you need to do is type in the title(The Protocols of the Learned Elders of Zion) and you will receive a plethora of webpages to choose from. I personally read them on the website: www.proletariatparty.wordpress.com

A copy of Henry Ford's "The International Jew" can be found there too. You can find them on the blog posts dated:

September 15, 2010 - for The International Jew, September 4, 2010 - for The Protocols of the Learned Elders of Zion(the post heading is "Are The Jews Really Plotting To Take Over The World"). And they may also be found at the top of the page if they have been reposted since then.

I will be giving a brief description of the book "The International Jew" in the next chapter. The website that I just referred you to is somewhat radical in the eyes of some, representing a socialist view and an uprising of the middle-class(or Proletariat) to take over the means of production for goods and services in The United States. They want to transfer the majority of the wealth from the elite 1 % of the country, to the working middle class people who produced it. I like that part of the movement and that's why I chose that website.

But back to the book. It generally states that the Jews of the world have conspired against every non-Jew on this planet to secretly control every aspect of their lives. In this book all non-Jew human beings are called "Goyim". Goyim is a word the elitists Jewish elders used to describe anyone that is not Jewish. The Protocols consist of 24 tenets and objectives that these Jewish leaders hope to, or are in the process of doing. So without further introduction here we go.

Protocol Number 1, Point 12, the Jewish elders say: *Our right lies in force. The word "right" is an abstract thought and proved by nothing. The word means no more than: Give me what I want in order that thereby I may have a proof that I am stronger than you.*

Point Number 16 states: *Let us, however, in our plans, direct our attention not so much to what is good and moral as to what is necessary and useful.*

These two points, show that in the Jewish culture there is no such thing as "right" and "wrong." The only thing that is important is that the Jew gets what he wants. There is evidence that shows the Jews don't treat each other like this, but when it comes to non-Jews everything is permissible and encouraged. In their eyes it is not wrong to rob or cheat a non-Jew, the only thing that is important is that the Jew gets what he wants and is satisfied. That means there is no limit to what the Jews are willing to do to you or anyone else to get what they want.

In Protocol Number 1, Point 23, The Jewish elders talk about their political beliefs:

Our countersign is - Force and Make-believe. Only force conquers in political affairs, especially if it be concealed in the talents essential to statesmen. Violence must be the principle, and cunning and make-believe the rule for governments which do not want to lay down their crowns at the feet of agents of some new power. This evil is the one and only means to attain the end, the good. Therefore we must not stop at bribery, deceit and treachery when they should serve towards the attainment of our end. In politics one must know how to seize the property of others without hesitation if by it we secure submission and sovereignty.

Here again in this Jewish Protocol it shows that anything is permissible, even in their wishes to control the world of politics. The passage states that violence and make-believe(lies) are acceptable tools to use in getting a nation or government to do what you want. Some people have accused Jews in America of attempting to influence American leaders into attacking Israel's enemies for them, by spreading lies and false intelligence reports. Some have said the United States was intentionally fed false information about Iraqi, Iranian, and Syrian weapons production in an attempt to make the U.S. attack these countries. All three of these countries are enemies of Israel, but don't have the

technical ability to be a threat to the U.S.A. This deceitful
rhetoric creates confusion in U.S. policy in hopes to make
us strike. I overheard someone say once, the Jews will not
rest until they make the U.S.A. attack and destroy all of
Israel's enemies. I've heard the Jews in America are not true
Americans at heart because the welfare of Israel is more
important to them than the safety, stability, and security
of the United States of America. As an example of the
confusion the President of Iran, Mahmoud Ahmadinejad,
has reportedly denied that the Jewish Holocaust during
World War II ever happen and that he wants to blow the
state of Israel off the face of the map. But as I stated earlier
there are over 25,000 Jews living in his country today
peacefully. I don't think a true Jew hater would allow that
to be. This creates confusion. Also, it has been said that Iran
is an enemy to the U.S.A., but Iran says they are only an
enemy of Israel and not the United States of America. This
also creates confusion. Which or what is the truth?

Protocol Number 2, Point 2, states : *The administrators,
whom we shall choose from among the public, with strict
regard to their capacities for servile obedience, will not be
persons trained in the arts of government, and will therefore
easily become pawns in our game in the hands of men of*

learning and genius who will be their advisers, specialists bred and reared from early childhood to rule the affairs of the whole world.

This is telling us that the Jews are choosing people they have hand-picked for Americans to vote for in a public government office. Jews are regulating our choices. They are giving us candidates that once elected are loyal to only them.

Protocol 2, Point 5, states that the Jews have taken over the media: *Through the press we have gained the power to influence while remaining ourselves in the shade; thanks to the press we have got the gold in our hands, notwithstanding that we have had to gather it out of the oceans of blood and tears. But it has paid us, though we have sacrificed many of our people. Each victim on our side is worth in the sight of God a thousand goyim.*

The Jews realized if they controlled the news, movies, radio, and print media they could control what version of history was told. What version of the future would be projected. Who is good and who is evil. What all this means is that they can control the world agenda. In this point you also see the arrogance of the Jews when they state that to them, one Jew is worth 1000 of us, non-Jewish human beings.

Protocol Number 3, Point 2, says: *We have made a gulf between the far-seeing sovereign power and the blind force of the people so that both have lost all meaning, for like the blind man and his stick, both are powerless apart.*

Here they are stating they have been successful in separating God from the people, and the people from God. What more can I say about that statement.

Some protocols look like a direct reflection of what we are going through in the world today economically without further explanation.

Protocol Number 3, Point 5, states : *All people are chained down to heavy toil by poverty more firmly than ever. They were chained by slavery and serfdom; from these, one way and another they might free themselves. These could be settled with, but from want they will never get away. We have included in the constitution such rights as to the masses appear fictitious and not actual rights. All these so-called "People's rights" can exist only in idea, an idea which can never be realized in practical life. What is it to the proletariat laborer, bowed double over his heavy toil, crushed by his lot in life, if takers get the right to babble, if journalists get the right to scribble any nonsense side by side with good stuff, once the proletariat has no other profit out of the constitution save only those pitiful crumbs which we fling them from our table in return for their voting in favor of what we dictate, in favor of the men we place in power, the servants of our Agentur... Republican rights for a poor man are no more than a bitter piece of irony, for the necessity he is under of toiling almost all day gives him no present use of them, but the other hand robs him of all guarantee of regular and certain earnings by making him dependent on strikes by his comrades or lockouts by his masters.*

Are we not in this country going through this exact problem. Our political commentators with big corporations on television attack unions. Wages are down, jobs are lost to go overseas, and the American people are told to shut up and continue to labor for the top 1% of the Jews and those non-Jews that have sold out and work of them.

In Protocol Number 3, Point 11, the Jews state how they will bring an economic crisis to everyone all over the world: *This hatred will be still further magnified by the effects of an economic crisis, which will stop dealing on the exchanges and bring industry to a standstill. We shall create by all the secret subterranean methods open to us and with the aid of gold, which is all in our hands, a universal economic crises whereby we shall throw upon the streets whole mobs of workers simultaneously in all the countries of Europe.*

Right now today as I'm writing this book, I watched on the television as workers are rioting in France. Gold is at its highest prices because of fear. The industry of manufacturing is at its lowest levels in years in the U.S.

Protocol Number 3, Point 12, goes on to say that Jewish money and economics will not be affected: *"Ours" they will not touch, because the moment of attack will be known to us and we shall take measures to protect our own.*

Right now, the Israeli government has sent out messages stating that Israel is one of the only countries today flourishing during these world economic troubles.

Protocol Number 3, Point 16,: *At the present day we are, as an international force, invincible, because if attacked by some we are supported by other states.*

Presently, Israel depends on the military might and power of the United States to deter and protect them from the majority, if not all of the countries in the Middle East and the surrounding areas.

Protocol Number 3, Point18 and 19, states: *Naturally they do not tell the peoples that this unification must be accomplished only under our sovereign rule. - And thus the people condemn the upright and acquit the guilty -* The Protocol goes on to say: *Thanks to this state of things, the people are destroying every kind of stability and creating disorders at every step.*

Protocol Number 5, points 2 and 4, These Protocols say the Jews will lead the masses of people with lies and misdirection: *We shall be told that such a despotism as I speak of is not consistent with the progress of these days, but I will prove to you that is. - Moreover, the art of directing masses and individuals by means of cleverly manipulated theory and verbiage, by regulations of life in common and all sorts of other quirks, in all which the goyim understand nothing, belongs likewise to the specialists of our administrative brain.*

Before World War II, it has been said that 3800 of 4500 lawyers in Germany were Jews. Also, the Germans felt like the Jews were robbing them and manipulating them. And during this time in Germany unemployment was at its highest levels hovering over 10%. Soon after the election of the National Socialists and the Jews were removed from positions of power, the unemployment rate dropped to almost at 0% thanks to projects like the German Autobaun.

Protocol 5, Points 5 and 6, states that the Jews are successfully turning all non-Jews against one another by inciting religious and racial hatred. The point goes on to later state that the Jews and those that work for the Jews control the Gold market and Gold itself.:

> *We have set one against another the personal and national reckonings of the Goyim, religious and racial hatreds, which we have fostered into a huge growth in the course of the past 20 centuries. This is the reason why there is not one State which would anywhere receive support if it were to raise its arm, for every one of them must bear in mind that any agreement against us would be unprofitable to itself. - It is through me that Kings reign - All the wheels of the machinery of all the states go by the force of the engine, which is in our hands, and that engine of the machinery of states is - (Gold).*

Protocol 5, Point 7, states that it is important to outlaw guns for the average citizen so they will be defenseless against the Jews: *Nowadays it is more important to disarm the peoples than to lead them into war;*

Protocol Number 5, Points 8,10,and 11, These points say that the Jews are giving the non-Jews a "Show" and are creating a state of mass confusion: *They are content with a show and rarely pause to note, in the public arena, whether promises are followed by performance. - In order to put public opinion into our hands we must bring it into a state of bewilderment by giving expression from all sides to so many contradictory opinions and for such length of time as will suffice to make the goyim lose their heads in the labyrinth and come to see that the best thing is to have no opinion of any kind in matters political, - that it will be impossible for anyone to know where he is in the resulting chaos, so that the people in consequence will fail to understand one another.* The Point goes on to say that they hate people that take their lives, circumstances, and fate of their country into their own hands. - *To discourage any kind of personal initiative which might in any degree hinder our affair. There is nothing more dangerous than personal initiative; if it has genius behind it, such initiative can do more than can be done by millions of people among whom we have sown discord.* Point 11 is powerful and finishes describing the Jews formation of their World Order or Super Government as the Protocols called it: *By all these means we shall so wear down the goyim that they will be compelled to offer us international power of a nature that by its position will enable us without any violence gradually to absorb all the state forces of the world and to form a super -government.*

Protocols Number 6, Points 1and 4, further explains how the Jews plan to dominate non-Jews economically by using banks to keep our land in debt: *We shall soon begin to establish huge monopolies, reservoirs of colossal riches, upon which even large fortunes of the goyim will depend to such an extent that they will go to the bottom together with the credit of the states on the day after the political smash... - at whatever cost to deprive them of their land. This object will be best attained by increasing the burdens upon landed property- in loading lands with debts.*

Protocol Number 6, Point 6, talks about how the Jews plan to use speculators to manipulate the stock market: *What we want is that industry should drain off from the land both labor and capital and by means of speculation transfer into our hands all the money of the world, and thereby throw all the goyim into the ranks of the proletariat. Then the goyim will bow down before us, if for no other reason but to get the right to exist.*

Protocol Number 7, Point 3, speaks about Israel's relationship with the countries around it: *We must be in a position to respond to every act of opposition by war with the neighbors of that country which dares to oppose us;*

Protocol Number 9, Point 10, describes the plan of the Jews to take control of educating the youth of the non-Jews: *We have fooled, bemused and corrupted the youth of the goyim by rearing them in principles and theories which are known to us to be false although it is that they have been inculcated.*

Protocol Number 10, Point 5, states that the Jews are systematically and purposefully, attempting to destroy non-Jewish families: *We shall destroy among the goyim the importance of the family and its educational value and remove the possibility of individual minds splitting off,*

Protocol Number 10, points 10 and 11, states the Jews capacity to appoint Presidents and political leaders. If this is true, is there anything that is real anymore? : *And then it was that we replaced the ruler by a caricature of a government - by a President, taken from the mob, from the midst of our puppet creatures, or slaves. - In the near future we shall establish the responsibility of Presidents.*

Protocol Number 15, point 10,mentions that the Jews are controlling congressmen: *Even Senators and the higher administration accept our counsels.*

Protocol Number 11, Point 7, The Jews claim to have set up the tenets and principles of Freemasonry, thereby controlling the institution from the upper echelons. They claim to have set up masonry as a control mechanism over the masses: *For what, indeed, if not in order to obtain in a roundabout way what is for our scattered tribe unattainable by the direct road? It is this which has served as the basis for our organization of secret masonry which is not known to, and aims which are not even so much as suspected by, these "Goy" cattle, attracted by us into the "Show" army of Masonic lodges in order to throw dust in the eyes of their fellows.*

Also protocol 15, Points 4 and 5 discusses Masonry : *For these lodges we shall find our principal intelligence office and means of influence - among the members of these lodges will be almost all the agents of international and national police*

- it is natural that we and no other should lead Masonic activities, for we know whither we are leading, we know the final goal of every form of activity whereas the goyim have knowledge of nothing not even of the immediate effect of action;

Protocol Number 12, Point 7, The Jews say they will attempt to stop books they don't like from being published.(Lord God, please let me find a publisher who has the strength to publish this book): *And if there should be any found who are desirous of writing against us, they will not find any person eager to print their productions. Before accepting any production for publication in print, the publisher or printer will have to apply to the authorities for permission to do so. Thus we shall know beforehand of all tricks preparing against us and shall nullify them by getting ahead with explanations on the subject treated of.*

Protocol Number 12, Point 12, The Jews claim they're in control of our political parties: *Those fools who will think they are repeating the opinion of a newspaper of their own camp will be repeating our opinion or any opinion that seems desirable for us. In the vain belief that they are following the organ of their party they will, in fact, follow the flag which we hang out for them.*

I just found it interesting that Protocol Number 13 starts off by saying: *The need for daily bread forces the goyim to keep silence and be our humble servants.* I believe that this is a very direct and profound statement.

Protocol Number 16, Point 1, describes the Jews abilities to control our teachers and Universities by controlling their lesson plans and teaching methods : *The universities, by reeducating them in a new direction their officials and professors will be prepared for their business by detailed secret programs of action from which they will not with immunity diverge, not by one iota. They will be appointed with the especial precaution, and will be so placed as to be wholly dependent upon the government.*

Now this I found very interesting and when I read it I was thoroughly shaken. The Jews claim to have changed the way our history has been written - Protocol Number 16, Point 4 : *Classicism as also any form of study of ancient history, in which there are more bad than good examples, we shall replace with the study of the program of the future. We shall erase from the memory of men all facts of previous centuries which are undesirable to us and leave only those which depict all the errors of the government of the goyim.*

Even right now, it is politically incorrect to speak against Jewish tyranny and the state of Israel, even if what you say is true and you have the facts to prove it. World history has been rewritten throughout the decades to make the Jews look favorable and to distort reality to the point where the truth no longer exists.

Protocol Number 17, Points 2 and 3, discusses the Jews plans to destroy the Christian church and also to go even a step further into the Catholic structure: *We have long past taken care to discredit the priesthood of the goyim, and thereby to ruin their mission on Earth which in these days might still be a great hindrance to us. Day by day its influence on the peoples of the world is falling lower. Freedom of conscience has been declared everywhere, so that NOW only years divide us from the moment of the complete wrecking of that Christian religion:*

Concerning Catholics Point 3 goes on to say: *When the time comes finally to destroy the papal court the finger of an invisible hand will point the nations towards this court. When, however, the nations fling themselves upon it, we shall come forward in the guise of its defenders as if to save excessive bloodshed. By this diversion we shall penetrate to its very bowels and be sure we shall never come out again until we have gnawed through the entire strength of this place.*

And in Protocol Number 17, Point 7, here the Jews describe how they are using the American intelligence agencies to spy on American citizens inside the U.S. *In our programs one-third of our subjects will keep the rest under observation from a sense of duty, on the principle of volunteer service to the state. It will then be no disgrace to be a spy and informer, but a merit*

Protocol Number 20, Points 20 and 31, These points further elaborate on the Jews plans to create economic crisis through a form of usury and selling the debt of nations like the United States to foreign interests in an attempt to bring a government under its control: *Economic crises have been produced by us for the goyim by no other means than the withdrawal of money from circulation. Huge capitals have stagnated, withdrawing money from states, which were constantly obliged to apply to those same stagnant capitals for loans. These loans burdened the finances of the state with the payment of interest and made them the bond slaves of these capitals…. The concentration of industry in the hands of capitalists out of the hands of small masters has drained away all the juices of the peoples and with them also the states - From this calculation it is obvious that with any form of taxation per head the state is baling out the last coppers of the poor taxpayers in order to settle accounts with wealthy foreigners, from whom it has borrowed money instead of collecting these coppers for its own needs without the additional interest.*

Protocol Number 21, Points 2 and 8, Explains how the Jews have used the Banking industry to institute a form of usury aimed at crippling an economy to force it under Jewish control : *We have taken advantage of the venality of administrators and slackness of rulers to get our moneys twice, thrice and more times over, by lending to the goy governments moneys which were not at all needed by the states. Could anyone do the like in regard to us?.... Therefore, I shall only deal with the details of internal loans. - I beg you to concentrate your particular attention upon this point and upon the following: nowadays all internal loans are consolidated by so-called flying loans, that is, such as have terms of payment more or less near. These debts consist of moneys paid into the savings banks and reserve funds. If left for long at the disposition of a government these funds evaporate in the payment of interest on foreign loans, and are placed by the deposit of equivalent amount of rents.*

That was one last point on how the Jews cause economic crisis for their own profit and also practice usury. I could go on and on showing you interesting and life-changing statements that I read in the Protocols of the Learned Elders of Zion, but really what you need to do is read the entire book for yourself. But I do want to leave you with this last little thought about the Protocols. Some have said including most Jews that the protocols false, But I would like to ask you one question. How much of what was written in the Protocols of the Learned Elders of Zion can be related to what we are going through economically and politically in this world today? Do the Protocols, which were written years ago, reflect on any of today's current events? And if the Jews are really controlling the interests of the world, would they ever admit it? Wouldn't they say that it is all lies what people are writing and saying about them. If the Protocols are true, would you expect the Jews and their puppets to come clean and honestly tell the truth about what they are doing? May common sense always prevail and we all be brought to the light.

Chapter XVI

A Brief Description of Henry Ford's The International Jew The World's Foremost Problem

In concerning the book "The International Jew" by Henry Ford, I don't think that it is necessary to go into as much detail as I did summarizing and the Protocols of the Learned Elders of Zion because the book overlaps on some subject matter that has already been covered.

The book called The International Jew is really a set of pamphlets put together to make the form. It was first published in a newspaper called "The Dearborn Independent," a paper owned by Henry Ford. Henry Ford was an inventor, an industrialist, and the founder of the Ford Motor Company. Although Mr. Ford is most famous for producing quality automobiles, he also was a highly in-depth intellectual. The book is groundbreaking material and its influence is still felt by people around the world especially in Egypt and Germany where it was a bestseller.

The main focus or central point that the book is trying to make is that every Jew is a liar, a thief, an oppressor, and an almost satanic creature in its actions. The book goes on to describe Jewish Imperialism, the influence on Russia, Jewish supremacy in the movie industry, Jewish control of the liquor industry, and Jewish control of precious metals. The International Jew is truly an insightful read. I think that God has blessed the mind of the writer and every reader that understands its meaning. I truly hope that every individual gets an opportunity to read it. The book " The International Jew" can be found all over the internet.

Chapter XVII

A Brief Description of Dostoyevskys' A Writer's Diary

Fyodor Dostoyevsky is best known for his novel called " Crime and Punishment", but I believe his most provocative and insightful book is "A Writers Diary". The book describes how Jewish usury preys and takes advantage of the poorest, weakest, and most vunerable people in our society. He implies that where ever the Jew goes they humiliate and inflick human misery on the people there. Dostoyevsky leads me to believe there is solely one trait that is the reason for the Jews actions throughout the centuries, and that one trait is "mercilessness." This book is an almost necessary read for all who search for knowledge and the truth. May God watch over and protect us.

Writer's Note

Putting together this book was really a labor of love. I often thought about all the people I wanted to help by getting the truth out through this book. The dissemination of honest information is paramount in todays climate. If it were not for my trips to Europe, Southeast Asia, Israel (post Nakba), and the Middleast as a whole I don't think I would have had the insight to write this book and hopefully I have passed it on to you. We don't talk about these issues as much as we should in the U.S. and hopefully this book will act as the match, that sparked the flame , that lit up the world for someone to see.

As the final solution to the worlds problems has yet to be found, we must never stop striving to find it. I believe that history tends to repeat itself if solutions are not found and problems are not resolved. I see strange parallels between the world today and the way it was at the beginning of the last century. High unemployment, civil unrest, political

/ corporate corruption, and the general feelings of most people that they are boxed in and constricted - throughout history these feelings have led to revolutionary changes. Lets hope for peace, wisdom, and knowledge. I hope this book made you think. Sometimes while listening to my favorite composer Wagner, I often layback and wonder if maybe Dostoyevsky, Henry Ford, and Nilus knew the truth many years ago and we have been just a few steps behind. May God protect me and preserve the writings of this book throughout today and future generations to come.

Good luck everyone and God bless!

Acknowledgments

I'd especially like to thank Dr. Joseph and H.H. for supporting me during some difficult circumstances. Since I returned from overseas I don't think I would have been able to accomplish my goals without you. To Wilathip, in the last couple of years we tried our best, but timing and good fortune did not can accompany us on our journey. To, Steven B. thanks for being there and good times are ahead of us. To Robin L, I love you and I wish that we could talk and see each other more. To Karl and H., you are like brothers to me and I thank God that he brought you into my life. To Camille D.J.R., It is because of you that I know how to write. Can you believe my life? I wish that you were here so that we could talk one more time, I miss you. To James R, what can I say that hasn't already been said, you have been a major influence on my life. To my aunts, uncles, cousins, and other family members, I love you guys and I can't wait to have a big family reunion for all of us reconnect. To James A., our dreams are coming true. Our time is now !

To my friends from my many travels

Heather J, thanks for being my sounding board and phone friend. To Rose F, you have got to be one of the most loving people in the world. To Eric C, thanks for being a good friend and always trying to uplift me. To Lawrence A, other than my grandfather, you have got to be the hardest working family man in the world, thanks for being a good friend. To Ben G, thanks brother and I can't wait to see you and have a talk about everything, we have a long friendship ahead of us. To John B, thanks for traveling with me and being a good friend, it got kinda shaky there didn't it at times. To Mahmoud, you are one of the most generous and good hearted people I have ever met. I hope God allows our friendship to prosper. To Chris K, I think I would try things differently if could. To Christoph, Saba, Jackie O, Terry H, Mayelin, Rizzia, Mitzy, Miriam, To Dan, To Paul, To Alexandria G, Rym, Riwa, Karim, Felina, Korey J, Rico, Aymen, and Carolien thanks for being with me along the roads of my travels and helping me experience life.

To Nay

What can I say other than I wish that you were here with me to celebrate God's good grace. I hope that you enjoy the book. I cannot wait to see you and hear your stories about what life has brought your way. You have truly been missed. The forces that led to our separation will be met with an equal to or greater than force that will bring our lives back into balance. Darkness will never prevail over us, God shines his light on the righteous and that's why you will always be seen. I love you until the ends of time and space.

To Jehu

Too much time has past and I hope this book finds you well and safe. You, just like a Supernova, are truly one of God's miracles that I don't see enough of. Since the first day that I met you on September 22, 2006 I knew that you were destined for greatness. I hope that you are increasing in knowledge and I cannot wait to share my experiences and insight with you. In a strange way that I cannot explain, had not time and oppositional forces dictated our current situation I might not have written this book. I hope to explain it to you someday. May this book be a guide for you to follow out of the labyrinth and into your calling. More than I can tell you now, the " powers that be" that are explained in this book have had a greater effect on your life than you realize or could possibly imagine. Regardless of what happens from here until eternity, I want you to know that I will always love you and may God watch over you and give you the strength and courage to endure. Until order is restored I can only have faith and believe that all things work for the good of those......